John Thomas Allen

Rolling in the Third Eye

SurVision Books

First published in 2020 by
SurVision Books
Dublin, Ireland
Reggio di Calabria, Italy
www.survisionmagazine.com

Copyright © John Thomas Allen, 2020

Design © SurVision Books, 2020

ISBN: 978-1-912963-15-7

This book is in copyright. No part of this publication may be reproduced, stored in a retrieval system, or transmitted in any form or by any means without the prior permission in writing from the publisher.

Acknowledgments

Grateful acknowledgment is made to the editors of the following, in which some of these poems, or versions of them, originally appeared:

Arsenic Poetry Journal: "Dust"

The Cimarron Review: "The Three Men and the Starfish"

DM du Jour: "Bitter Fruit" and "Death"

The Eighth Street Publishing Guild: "The Red Letter"

Grey Sparrow Journal: "Go to the Graveyard but Whisper"

HelloHorror: "The Lighthouse above the Graveyard"

The Literary Hatchet: "Fatherhood"

Lumiere: "Misheard" and "Dry Ophelia"

SurVision: "Nightshade Lullaby," "The Old Age of the Assassins," and "Dilate"

To Alejandra Pizarnik (1936–1972)
Cecilia McGough, Astronomer
Andy Younkins
Dr. L

Contents

Amor Fati	5
Bitter Fruit	6
The Mice	7
The Block Train	8
Camphor Body	10
Dilator	12
The Blue Spaces	14
Dry Ophelia	15
Dust	16
Fatherhood	17
Visiting Hours	18
Go to the Graveyard but Whisper	19
Nightshade Lullaby	20
The Old Age of the Assassins	21
The Purple Emperor's Astral Rotation	22
The Three Men and the Starfish	24
The Lighthouse above the Graveyard	25
Lunaire's Village	26
Marlene	28
Misheard	29
Purity	30
The Red Letter	32
The Distance of a Rose	34
Roswell Construction	36
The Yellow Jester	37
Epilogue: The Cufflinks of Dream	38

Amor Fati

Death, come not cheaply. Neither in blue coma
or wrinkled hints of somatization; spin in a noir

parapet of black hats, squeeze me with Mitchum's
preacher hand, thick and meaty; let each

sound be a music box's last gold pluck. Death,
come not cheaply, wind up as a music box,

fall as its last symphony. Come in a black hat,
tattooed and preachy or stay home and

make a strange color of me, as Martha and Mary's
pale brother waiting in his Father's light
house for instructions, olive green eyes,

staring past us forever.

Bitter Fruit ("Tantalus Breaking")

All day I watch and play
my bruised viola; I care nothing
for fruit, and haven't in years. I
compose atop bone split rock,
grease skull mounts wrung oil saps,
scream and blister flame.
All noon I watch a yellow
tide rise with berry pimpled
screams, rot temptation.

Let it stink to high heaven.

The Mice

After Georg Trakl

Into the brick abandoned house the tired mice run.
Curious slivers of moonlight peek in.
Icy wind scatters pages of black leaves
from an old Bible left on the floor.

Pink bellied and starving, they devour Acts 2:1.
A percussion of white squeaks begin.
In the demolished ribcage of dirty brick,
their eyes shine like dogs in wet moonlight.

Smoke belches from their little mouths:
Pained and pentecostal, they know truth.
He watches from a broken window upstairs.
Damp echoes, footsteps, move slowly down.

The mice chase him as I reach a splintered landing.

The Block Train

Waking in a sand blast of bad sleep,
past a blinded Sphinx

I hear the chalkboard scream
of a pigeon yard dying as bars
slam through orange,

making the same sound
as teeth rubbing against stone.

I know one thing certainly
as ever; I am inheriting

these narcotic stems
of your deliberate dementia
cell by cell. For want
of ritual plastic burns,
kool aid lip balm, mop wigs

bored with sharp origami
games in a men's colony

You pause
a moment in record time

To fingerpaint a wail
you still hold
like a pastel tattoo
beneath the eye, kitsch
being contempt's algae

as a train, and the bars' shadow
breezes by in one Rorschach spill,

with my head smudged
in one hexagonal smatter.

You always loved our
Aztec books at Christmas,

the gloss of limp prey
down estuary steps,

And here I am in these
In civilization's dual temples

killing time, wailing
with a Sacred Heart
wrapped
in your barbed wire.

Camphor Body

What I was missing you found.

A poster in a desolate city
city cell frequented by bus monks.

Where I undid an old girl's
orchid beads rotting in her curls

and rubbed Frankincense
on her mice bitten Book of Hours.

You had no time to search for me

especially during the day,

so your tarot, painted in 8mm
Took on a life of its own

extended in frames. I slept
in bathhouses and the Pollock displays,

the Hematite between your teeth pinched
the clocks of weather balloons I'd

captured and a lunar bleach
made me slick for your arms.

I came home after dealing cards
with old clowns in the library's reading

room. One, in a MOV only half
filmed, whispering lust, lust...

His eyes were toad jade, either/or,
a distant ore in a flapjack. Smearing my

lips with Dramamine, I dab away
continents in chemical paintings. I am

whole in your GIFS, your photo
formula, back in your darkroom. You will

add chilly organ spells to my adventures.
I am him now, her, the sex

of that trinity.

Dilator

These balustrades are sick and dizzy
and ring still with the echoes of your falling:

the song, distance, and symmetry.

Your mouth a stripped accordion
teeth strewn on marble like crushed chalk

I was away drilling doll catheters in place,
sweating nightmare goo in memory foam
the revolving chambers fired in dream soil

by leashed lobsters missing their daytime naps
and this through crack smoked hour glasses,

smeared motel keys, the rhizome fields of gag teeth
knocking in the slipping galleys of our plight

And here now we are wound bits
of motion sickness, moons in staring clocks,

Radio Flyers filled with Garbage Pail Kids rolling
over limbo borders, incinerated in their rear views.

And now these burning deja vu treaties,
these 3:00am tin masses like a rain

dancer's dream, beads filled in a chalice
and dribbling alien spunk on Chinese lanterns

white out for Heraclitean growth in reverse
for the tawny arrangements made in ouija coffins,

this ascetic birdsong of graveyards.

The Blue Spaces

For Candace Hilligos

In most spaces the blue won't hurt you;
the endless sky
will seem an unending beacon
akin to a never-ending bird
or simply an overfull pail.
In other spaces it will function as an x ray
baring your insides to all passerby
whether you notice or not.
The smaller they get, the more they seem
like small chinks in a prison half invisible,
a parable glued to shadow.
In the very rare spaces you will move
as a tired stranger might
aware of this horrible enormity,
this dislocated enmity
and find how small and without reality you are
in this origami puzzle,
this imprisoning infinite without end.

Dry Ophelia

unformed and anonymous,
urgently pinched in waves of finned dispersion

In the painting above the rocking chair
a distant face streaming slowly apart

in the slumping waves, a forgotten pond
a thin river

dry Ophelia, unsure where to fade
carrying bouquets neither real nor artificial
a symbiotic petal's haze
christening a sleeping sea
with clear blushes even
you don't understand
in the rocking chair
dry as the brush
you were painted with
still not knowing as
your sharp cheeks
strike the canvas

My dry Ophelia

Dust

Smoking patio
breathing pine bush
leaves of green razor.

The March leaf hanging like a crippled
butterfly—

A starless morning,
the cuffed breeze,
a sky's crisp condescension,
the blueness of your monster:

To speak in taxidermy,
empty sound bytes,
Christabel feathers

ringing in fall..

your mouth reeling celluloid
stuffed with black feathers. I
will not see you long again, it
should grow dark tonight.

You will talk your way back into it.

Fatherhood

I hypnotized the dream doll
it came yesterday.
The soft pickle hands, the big eyes
I could touch its dreaming
Its hands gnarled
In a vacant hothouse strewn with metal orchids
It came with a dream catheter miles long, uncouth
It was there I began to worship
I could hear it breathe
I came to be the templar
A vanguard for its hollowness
It was a matter of looking after—
I was there the night the eyes opened
glowing as a marquee rotten with light.
The pink lids grew swollen
I felt the vegetable heads bloom.
Such are the processes
with the poetic peony of birth
where a star sits fed by fruit flies
where its dream unfolds as a membrane
to feel the point the shade has
its horrible center
In our embrace
in the full hothouse growth
of my vegetable head

Visiting Hours

I will write you in the dream ministry
and the yellow ledger it has on
each bit of fractal magic passed
in the apple of Adam's eye, now sleeping.
These porch skeletons and the flowers
they hatch on your deserted moon villa,
on the song you whisper in a siren's tune,
the kindle of an Arabian fire and the phantasy light
sleeping on the church lawns.
I will unroll Aladdin's blanket,
hand on the visiting hour
awaiting the time you attend,
in the green lit skulls rising
in the drumroll ministries
in the drop hour by hour
in this half chill, a perfumed haunting.
And this is where hours of visitation grow
a perfumed blade of the uncouth,
the voodoo penicillin wrapped in tags
around your neck. Arnim's blue spider
bites, and in its web I sink,
I struggle, your friend's hands
with headdresses of incense, the noir
haunting for which you had
to go so far beneath the ground.
And this is the hour

Go to the Graveyard, but Whisper

If with your living hand
a flush melody all aces
you would wash the moss
from my stone I should blush,
blinking. My face has color now,
they whisper. Look. Sit with me
this one time, eyes lit with floral
runes. I have a suit and money,
quarters like moons over my eyes.
Can I have all of you for a moment?
Come closer. Look. Hear the dead
choir, ill, wailing; pick the ivy orbs,
leave a holly trail. Fear nothing.
My face has color now.

Nightshade Lullaby

Oh I've had enough of these ambulatory angels
Screaming ingots spun
in our ivory maiden's Cyclops' eye.

A crypt cuckoo tower
with sarcophagus marble
Eyes shark dead and self assured

stitched a flea bitten cat o nine tails

Oh I've had enough ambulatory angels
our universal children throwing lipstick

To the needy who hear crib death
and roast beneath the sarcophagus' cracked tower

eyes shark dead and self assured

Soft as a pearl bitten cat o nine tail;
verse is pyrite's finish, raining dayglo
The meadows rifled with bodiless déjà vu.

Pure music is the cry for a shepherd's mercy.

The Old Age of the Assassins

I have seen the Orient retire
In the pond's Yellow home base
I have seen the mothman with a gas mask,
his leather jacket opens to a candelabra
a nestle harmonium the nipples of Christmas
lights irradiate with crystal tenebrae.
I've tapped the split moonlight in reverberate
fractals and clipped the moon's plasma
with markered fevers, spells
 the snow's Symbolist moon
accruing a cache of pyrite bullets; the moon trapped
in fireflies and the crack smoked hourglass.
The trap peacock is spread eagle
in the Lego's eye, the sutured moon,
the sensory pheromones
and sixth senses.
I have seen the Orient retire cue balls
Through the brouhaha of the Leprechaun's
golden eyes traced in the breath
of a psychotic moon.
The phalanx Eskimos give unction
from on high
A spell traced in vision, lit with fever;
A.E.'s skull centers in flame.

The Purple Emperor's Astral Rotation

> *"For in my present life, I was pledged to the butterfly-winged Purple Emperor, against whom that tatterdemalion pretender, the king in yellow, eternally warred for possession of the Throne of Time/Space*
>
> *And we were entering an astrological cycle in which it was foretold that a king could over- throw an emperor..."*
>
> —William Patrick Murray, "The Purple Emperor"

dueling shadow parapets,
segmented hieroglyphs simmer in granulate
pearls flown together in a magnetic field
run cool with the brooks of space's canopy
and a hershey leather star pail, the big dipper's amethyst
dig. Sheetmetal codexes spin on a record player's
needle drooling with morphine tears frozen.
"Go grease the horse on the polident farm",
the dictation rolls, "the piano wire is holding
the blotters together,
"and peach warm her grin is stubble
with geode and harmonic gold." The
banjo insects laughter is split in ivory nubs,
cackling in the dark, Mr. Peanut nursing her
wounds in the silo, closing his eyes.
The dawn is capped bouillon
grinning, the steamed dawn
chilled in choral ice architecture,
the chilled pantomime leering down.

A blotter face rises also in the violin grottoes,
the nude wired mummy lies in the dentist's chair with
chinesefortune wax melting through a
burning color of halogen numbers, a lexical glossalia.
Artificially tanned, Sun Ra turns to me,
laughing. "Dictation ends," The cylinders
in Rutger Hauer's gun are filled with pearl mummy
teeth, each crag reflecting a pinched
strata of crystal light, Billy the Kid's smile
undone in these gallery's representation.
A drooling angel drops Kodak bits of 8mm
that move as stained glass dropsy in the captain's
sliced palm, rising and fading in the ship's darkroom.
The Icelandic Moss string through
the dead nun's midnight hour beads; they sink
in flanked procession with electronic candles
cinched in the riverbeds, fleets drowning in
an abortive mission. Slender man, a lettuce head,
bends as a chalk martyr, uncrowning himself,
drowns in the Instagram pond full of
garland Hosannas. The grated Tron guillotine
metal falls in the REM mirror, and Poe's head
appears as you unclutch the handle
two quarters sown in his eyes.
His fainting candelabras are bursting
with green Goblin flames, snaking in a Cthulu dance
the voodoo beads spin in the singed sigils,
the small PacMan domes blowing in trapdoor glass,
a sound as a xylophone skating is made, and expires
as the stars do, only here. Blue rain falls in seashell calypsos spun
as the glass trapdoor shatters and The Purple Empress: cries
asking why we watch her, we the hypnotized denizens
of a drowning dream!"

The Three Men and the Starfish

The windows were tapping Morse code,
each traced outside the glass.
The knock came as a slinky feather, purple.
The feather, a sea fish, beating as a heart
might with scales of golden ministry.
In the cotillion angles a showman blew in,
but that was the magician tracing
his name in lunar glass.
He waved, broke out sweatin,
his face pale like a whore in church.
I got lost, his three hands winding
The three doves on fire.
Now all the fish were colored laid out on blocks
The priest put a coin in the fish's mouth.
The shore man shot him with a flare gun,
I took the axe and split the emergency glass.
I said to what was there:

The words you heard
when the windows tapped
were not mine in their red tensile,
in their ring nostril hooves.
I said to what sat beside me:

This is an 8mm painting
of the Trinity,

and I am drowning in it.

The Lighthouse above the Graveyard

I am the keeper, the manager
of dim-wick ammonia. Blue goblets

rage at noontide, varicose flowers
bloom; an old woman's leg

walking to kneel. I wind solvents
for yard lines running in butterfly wings,

tracing their crippled beats,
keeping score. Pure iodine

and enunciate palmistry
(along with a little love)

is what keeps my sedate island
in good order. Bumps in the sand

knock and knock; I get around
most nights. It can be beautiful

watching the tide
kiss our namesakes away

Lunaire's Village

    I was ungluing her psychotropic
      sea glass brassiere,
      her robe of Tarot cane.
   Her orange lips parted
   and swollen moonflowers
   blew like black pollen
     with the geisha's
         drowned syllables
         her
          blue
           spider's
          moon psalm
            stained with humming algae
            and the floral arrangement's march
              of yellow sight.

   With a mellifluous cackle
     of bending gum ministries,
   her denture crowns
        spun in the roulette
 of cathode rays
 spelunking for ruined fortunes
   for cyclical shade
 of burning servants on cracked Roman Marble
 and ticking nights in trace paper rooms
 the transit opal of dark cherry eyes
and reptilian death rattles
   in columns of amphibian night jade.

      Thus it was that the noir dew
      spun in beady halls of peeping
      Venus flytraps and the deaf
      gloss eclipsing
           lunar lobotomies,
               cannibal stars
falling as asbestos on holiday,
     and the drowsy hitchers wept
clown tears
                    of twilight serum

Marlene

Marlene's rosary beads hung from
flaking skin which seemed
Peeling wallpaper, the flames
of a grand guignol. Handing me a tiny
newspaper, *"The Daily Bread"*,
she seemed surprised with rolling
eyes that I could quote Christ.
She spoke in slurring avenues, dissipation
through which the martyrs seemed
to scream. *Your tears, I say, are
hard and diamond, but my own alchemy
is too weak to wipe them away.* She swayed
back and forth in her chair
like a chicken, gazing through
vistas of smoke laced divinity.
Maybe when she held those
pipes she felt a little bit
closer to God. *"She smoked herself
silly,"* my roommate said with
fearful contempt. Perhaps this
is true, though her swaying
carried me between heaven and hell.

Misheard

The quietly spoken syllable.
you heard my name called
from now on *in paregoric,*
now you read only the letters that
stretch my skin into a private alphabet
a hanging hound of conscious intent
a jaw plaque of imaginary vowels.
blurry and unclear.
I put mouth to deaf ears
ear to mute mouth
In the hope you'll say
my entirety.

Purity

The dead are painless and in pure spirit
they float, crucified, on matchsticks;
cubby whispers and punctured IV bags
dribble with baby hearts beating
war hymns. Their faces suspend
as orphan moons, necrotic jackals howl

and jeweled lesions bare in the stinky
grin of stray puppet bodies bound
to barbed, straw crosses. In the fields
trespassers are punished, nailed to oars
and spun like Goldilocks to face their stature
the thirsty soil slaked by its sorrow.

Moonflowers blow in vacant sentries.
The reeds lit dimly with their gaslight,
blow the pale wind song of young consumptives
     blowing paddles on the River Styx
to echo the widowed nursery rhymes'
stripped melody of burning ogatwas.

I started going to Mass in the winter.
The monstrance raised filled with moon
and found me in the back, a pair of eyes
rolling in the dark. I whispered that
     even *Lazarus will die as a responsorial*
psalm, eating my Host slowly.
He will be dead, holy, filled with star lice,
battered and blue as fanged wheat, vital

rising in plague wheat and heavy
with the weight of joined arms
in nodding mezzos and hypnosis trinities.
The dead's eyes are loose and gentle
filled with the season's marrow
egg white in nostril shock,
they crawl, the circus dogs
the growling hounds in perpetual pause.
    Their bottled tears are the solvent
  for the wheel squeak of stillborn carriages
   and solution a fungal vertebrae,
   the solvent for sudden clowns
     for a trickster gods' embrace,
   and the rain bled sloth
     of carnival dirges.

The Red Letter

For Julianne Buschbaum

Amnesia is this pocket serum sacrament
blown in darts by dawn from the waking saints

now this sunrise split as perforate tissue,
this elision spilling as on a burnt canvas. *I've*

had my nonconsensual experiences
A creeping Gilman yellow, slow as subatomic

parcels, chutes lateral in jeweled stars
to dust the tongues of snowblowers

in the stagnant oasis of your Fargo home.
Life goes on, yeah, until it doesn't any longer

Antibodies spun in fool's gold hold to
sugar angels arches; her steady rocking

chair, a siren's inverse call, Dickinson's nightshade,
hair ribbons; a body and its release in a mosque

of scalped neon, anonymity's rented rooms.

Rocking chair flooded, shadow spindle
wood, locked sighs in paint's drying point.

Downcast you pulled acoustic chlorine's
loose guns to no effect. Bodiless you wove

in the Red Letter sewn to a target, notes
of a glass violin always closer. I've had

my nonconsensual experiences.
Our Icarian forceps leak away as diurnal shadow

to a sick purr, with flypaper music
bars hold the grooves, white star bits falling
in webbed geometry. And here the sown ivy

of your earthbound bed, the pigeons trailing
as if to mourn, as though to say:

*My absence you
cannot argue with.*

The Distance of a Rose

In the moon was a girl who played
the starfish notes of an astral organ,
a Masonic filigree sewn on the jackboots
of those who came to reign
in nightmare galleys, glass constellates
who came to replace wonder with rude
splashes of green.

I left it with you
the clown's blush that swelters
on your city window, the cribbed
notes from your quiet genocide,
carried away in the spotted noon
by a lark, maybe, or some lexical
hummingbird. The glower I wear
now is an appraisal of this chipped
birdhouse—this world without you.

The cupboards, the spoons, the rain;
all alone, the little girl enjoying the yard:
on these days your small eyes
grew as orbs powered by rocket fuel,
and I know this well. In each was a heart
through which my heart has seized, at least,
if not stopped. Chaos begins syllabic—
a splash, an echo, then the full run
till you can't hear yourself
above a sundial's uproar.

The deposits your innocence makes;
your olive eyes, space's love deposits,
will leak by and by. The carnies, belly
dancers, the capital grind will eat
from within, where the innocent dead
have been placed like room keys.

The looping mandalas will twine
above the city, the radar of your
corruption will grow with the diamond
harvest, or some form
of limbic prison
where you straddle the heavens
but never touch the angels.

Roswell Construction

In the desert
we wear tinfoil caps

As it grows warmer
The beads spill down our faces
bits of a rock salt rosary

Breaks are taken
when it rains

for sand dune novenas
We drink and pray to mosaics
made eyeless by white sand

sandblasted by lattice waves
Light congregates
on each man's head

from one altitude to the next
above and below
endlessly

The Yellow Jester

(Robert W. Chabers)

His face expands in oblong midnight,
the base of each point dissolving
in black mother-of-pearl pools.

His fingernails wind round synaptic
pipe cleaners in the brain's contorting
base, and in nightmares his pillars stand

rude with moonlight. Angels with narcotic
eyes roll in stone orbs of ether, and tiles
of trick satin rife with purple fuzz,

gangrenous as his rumor, pull back
in your drowning to reveal him,
leering, jaundiced, teeth numbered

in hexes of ashen cuneiform spinning
as your breast heaves once more,
and a sign forms in Yellow.

Epilogue

The Cufflinks of Dream

The poet's job is to go on holding on to something like faith,
through the darkness of total lack of faith... the eclipse of God.

—David Gascoyne

Incantatory insouciance,
suffocating speeches,
futile tracts

Revolt as University parlor game,
anarchic intellects spun into coma,
the flirtation with fascism where our eyes
are exchanged for another's,
illuminations gone.

The marvelous stands on life support,
technocrat supercorporate archivists
lock away our imaginal zones, conscience
deemed mad by diviners of only the dollar
joy's anarchic estuary stilled by bitter hearts,
blood diamond merchants, the military moratoriums,
peacetime patriotism:
that silent pact for a corpse's amnesia.

In this sterile hothouse where Eros is monitored at every level,
let us renew our alien covenant: to water Novalis' blue flower
to fashion strange aeons from astral hydrangea,
Aegean moon ministries in spectral ballrooms,
to leave everything, to fashion the alchemy of the word
in crowned phrases hushed on triptych sound mirrors
over and above
our policed and policing world's death drive.

More poetry published by SurVision Books

Noelle Kocot. *Humanity*
(New Poetics: USA)
ISBN 978-1-9995903-0-7

Ciaran O'Driscoll. *The Speaking Trees*
(New Poetics: Ireland)
ISBN 978-1-9995903-1-4

Helen Ivory. *Maps of the Abandoned City*
(New Poetics: England)
ISBN 978-1-912963-04-1

Elin O'Hara Slavick. *Cameramouth*
(New Poetics: USA)
ISBN 978-1-9995903-4-5

John W. Sexton. *Inverted Night*
(New Poetics: Ireland)
ISBN 978-1-912963-05-8

Afric McGlinchey. *Invisible Insane*
(New Poetics: Ireland)
ISBN 978-1-9995903-3-8

Anatoly Kudryavitsky. *Stowaway*
(New Poetics: Ireland)
ISBN 978-1-9995903-2-1

Tim Murphy. *The Cacti Do Not Move*
(New Poetics: Ireland)
ISBN 978-1-912963-07-2

Tony Kitt. *The Magic Phlute*
(New Poetics: Ireland)
ISBN 978-1-912963-08-9

Clayre Benzadón. *Liminal Zenith*
(New Poetics: USA)
ISBN 978-1-912963-11-9

Thomas Townsley. *Tangent of Ardency*
(New Poetics: USA)
ISBN 978-1-912963-15-7

George Kalamaras. *That Moment of Wept*
ISBN 978-1-9995903-7-6

Anton Yakovlev. *Chronos Dines Alone*
(Winner of James Tate Poetry Prize 2018)
ISBN 978-1-912963-01-0

Bob Lucky. *Conversation Starters in a Language No One Speaks*
(Winner of James Tate Poetry Prize 2018)
ISBN 978-1-912963-00-3

Christopher Prewitt. *Paradise Hammer*
(Winner of James Tate Poetry Prize 2018)
ISBN 978-1-9995903-9-0

Mikko Harvey & Jake Bauer. *Idaho Falls*
(Winner of James Tate Poetry Prize 2018)
ISBN 978-1-912963-02-7

Tony Bailie. *Mountain Under Heaven*
(Winner of James Tate Poetry Prize 2019)
ISBN 978-1-912963-09-6

Nicholas Alexander Hayes. *Amorphous Organics*
(Winner of James Tate Poetry Prize 2019)
ISBN 978-1-912963-10-2

John Bradley. *Spontaneous Mummification*
(Winner of James Tate Poetry Prize 2019)
ISBN 978-1-912963-13-3

Gary Glauber. *The Covalence of Equanimity*
(Winner of James Tate Poetry Prize 2019)
ISBN 978-1-912963-12-6

Maria Grazia Calandrone. *Fossils*
Translated from Italian
(New Poetics: Italy)
ISBN 978-1-9995903-6-9

Sergey Biryukov. *Transformations*
Translated from Russian
(New Poetics: Russia)
ISBN 978-1-9995903-5-2

Alexander Korotko. *Irrazionalismo*
Translated from Russian
(New Poetics: Ukraine)
ISBN 978-1-912963-06-5

Anton G. Leitner. *Selected Poems 1981–2015*
Translated from German
ISBN 978-1-9995903-8-3

All our books are available to order via
http://survisionmagazine.com/books.htm